THE LEGENDARY FACE-OFF

ODIN

VS

ARES

by Lydia Lukidis

CAPSTONE PRESS
a capstone imprint

Published by Capstone Press, an imprint of Capstone.
1710 Roe Crest Drive, North Mankato, Minnesota 56003
capstonepub.com

Library of Congress Cataloging-in-Publication Data is available
on the Library of Congress website
ISBN: 9781669016502 (hardcover)
ISBN: 9781669016458 (paperback)
ISBN: 9781669016465 (ebook PDF)

Summary:
It's time for two gods of war to clash! The Norse god Odin is the Allfather and
the god of war. He uses his wisdom to guide him in combat strategy. Meanwhile,
Ares, the Greek god of war, uses his brute strength and fighting skills to be an
unstoppable force in battle. If these two gods faced off on the battlefield, who
would come out on top?

Editorial Credits
Editor: Aaron Sautter; Designer: Bobbie Nuytten; Media Researcher: Rebekah
Hubstenberger; Production Specialist: Whitney Schaefer

Image Credits
Alamy: AF Fotografie, 25, Chronicle, 11, 23, Ivy Close Images, 4, 15; Getty
Images; benoitb, 26, Hulton Archive, 21, mikroman6, 13, THEPALMER, 19;
National Gallery of Art: Pepita Milmore Memorial Fund, 17; Shutterstock:
Bourbon-88, 27, Gilmanshin, 5, 29, itechno, cover (bottom right), Kalleeck, 13, 14,
Liliya Butenko, 7, 8, Morphart Creation, 9, Natalia Mikhalchuk, cover (top left),
28; The New York Public Library: Miriam and Ira D. Wallach Division of Art,
Prints, and Photographs, 16

All internet sites appearing in back matter were available and accurate when this
book was sent to press.

Printed and bound in China. PO5379

TABLE OF CONTENTS

Words in **bold** are in the glossary.

TWO GODS OF WAR COLLIDE

WHOOSH!

An eight-legged, winged horse zooms across the night sky. An old man wearing a blue cloak rides the horse. When the moon shines on his face, it's clear he has only one eye.

Meet the god Odin, the Allfather. He is the head of the Norse **pantheon**. The Norse people are also called Vikings. Odin is the god of war and death. He also stands for wisdom, magic, and poetry.

Odin

Suddenly, a flash of fire pierces the air. The fire comes from four horses lugging a chariot. Ares steers the chariot. He clutches his spear and shield proudly.

Ares is the Greek god of war and destruction. He is known for being beast-like and a fierce fighter. But he also stands for courage and decisiveness.

Which of these gods of war is more powerful? Who has more abilities? Will Odin or Ares be the one to come out on top? Let the battle begin!

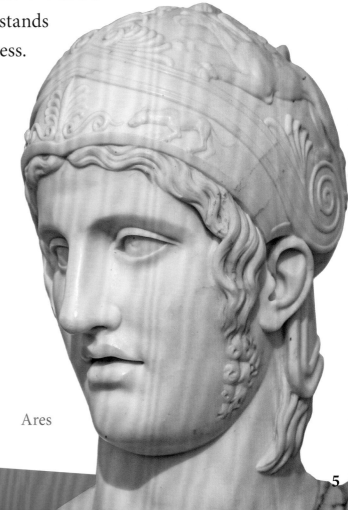

Ares

A long time ago, fire and ice came together in the **primordial** world. According to Norse myths, there were no gods or people yet. But one day, the giant Ymir came into being.

A cow named Audhumla also sprang forth from the fire and ice. To survive, Ymir drank the cow's milk. The cow fed herself by licking salt from the stones.

Then one day, POOF! Buri, the first Norse god, freed himself from the salt. In time, Buri had a son named Borr, who went on to marry Bestla. Together they had three godly children: the chief god Odin and his brothers Vili and Ve.

The huge giant Ymir and Audhumla the cow
were the first beings to exist in Norse myths.

As an important god, Ares has an equally important dad—Zeus. Zeus is the leader of the **Olympian** gods. He's the big boss. He was first married to the goddess Metis. But Zeus was not a loyal husband. He grew bored and left Metis to marry Hera.

Together, Zeus and Hera had three children. One was Ares.

Zeus

But things are a bit
complicated. Hera is actually
Zeus's sister! That means Hera
is Ares's mother and also his aunt.
In Ancient Greece, it wasn't unusual
for brothers and sisters
to get married.

Hera

GODLY STRENGTHS

Odin is a powerful god of war and death. It is said he cannot lose a battle. One of his strengths is using **strategy** in war. This is unlike Ares, who simply delights in destruction.

Norse warriors call upon Odin during times of war. They ask for his wisdom and special gifts. According to some Viking tales, Odin decides which battles will be successful.

Odin also decides which warriors will live or meet their end in combat. He chooses which warriors deserve to go to Valhalla. The **Valkyries** help Odin. The Valkyries are supernatural warrior women. They guide the chosen warriors to Valhalla after death.

Viking Paradise

Valhalla is a beautiful palace in the afterlife. Rows of spears support the roof that is covered with warriors' golden shields. Each night, the warriors sit at long banquet tables for the feast that Odin provides. The gates of Valhalla are said to be so wide that 800 warriors can walk through them side by side. Wolves guard the hall's gates while eagles fly above.

Odin isn't the only god of war. Ares is too. In fact, Ares is **brutal**. Few warriors, if any, can match his level of skill in combat. The Greek goddess, Athena, uses wisdom and strategy in battle, much like Odin. But Ares doesn't care for strategy. He just wants to fight.

Ares' physical aggression is one of his strengths. Of all the Greek gods, Ares is the most destructive. The ancient Greek poet Homer compares many heroes to Ares.

FACT

Sparta is a city in Ancient Greece dedicated to war. The Spartans honor Ares as the model soldier and a symbol of manly virtue.

Ares is skilled with all weapons. But he's known mostly for his sword and spear. He carries them at all times so he's always ready for battle.

In battle, Ares was skilled with both the spear and the sword.

Odin isn't just a skilled warrior. He's also known for his wisdom. As the smartest of the Norse gods, he has a thirst for knowledge. This gives him an advantage over his opponents.

FACT

Some of Odin's knowledge comes from his pet ravens, Huginn and Muninn. He sends them out into the world every morning and they return every night. They tell him about everything they see.

There was only one wiser then Odin—his uncle Mimir. According to myth, Odin learned that Mimir gained wisdom by drinking from a special well. When Odin realized the magical waters helped Mimir see the future, he set off to find the well. When he did, he asked permission to drink from it. Mimir said he could. But he warned Odin that he would have to pay a big price.

To drink from the well, it would cost Odin an eye. He agreed and gouged one of his eyes right out of its socket. Then, PLOP! He tossed it into the well. That allowed him to use the magical water and gain its **divine** wisdom.

Odin went to Mimir to ask for great wisdom.

Ares isn't just strong and fierce. He has other qualities that make him a great warrior. He's brave, for one. He fought in wars against both the Titans and the giants. Ares is decisive and fearless, and always willing to take a risk. He once killed a giant named Mimas. Mimas was a vicious fighter, with a tail full of serpents.

Ares also played an important role in the Trojan War. He had the courage to go against the Olympic gods. Most of them fought for the Greeks. Ares sided with the Trojans to support his girlfriend, Aphrodite. Ares often found himself at odds with his half-sister, Athena. But that didn't bother him. He wasn't afraid of her, or anyone else.

Ares and Athena sometimes fought against each other during times of war.

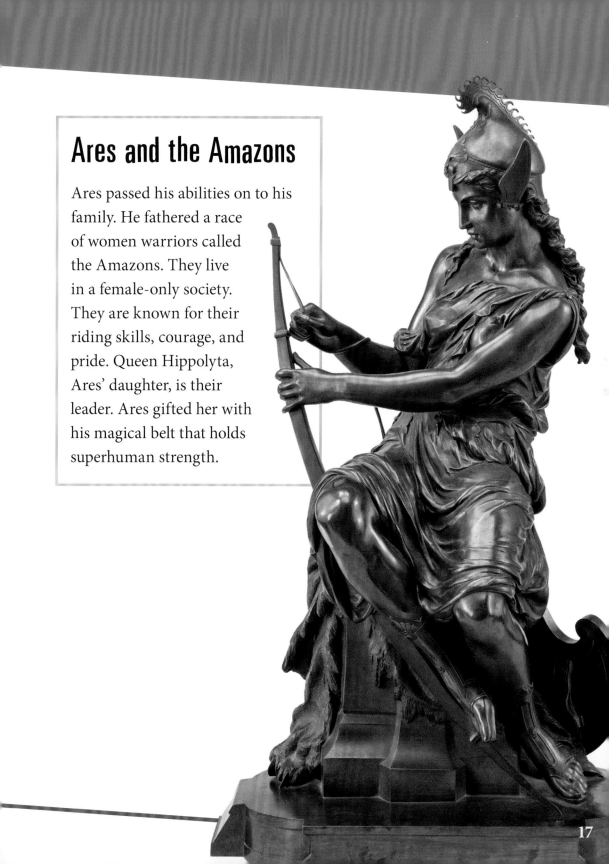

Ares and the Amazons

Ares passed his abilities on to his family. He fathered a race of women warriors called the Amazons. They live in a female-only society. They are known for their riding skills, courage, and pride. Queen Hippolyta, Ares' daughter, is their leader. Ares gifted her with his magical belt that holds superhuman strength.

ASTOUNDING POWERS

Both gods possess fantastic powers. For example, Odin has great magical abilities. He performs magic spells that give him **foresight**.

Odin can do other magical things too. He can heal others and communicate with spirits. He can calm storms and turn weapons against his attackers. He can even put a spell on others to make them do what he wants. In one myth, he put a sleeping spell on one of the Valkyries.

Odin once performed a **ritual** to gain the knowledge of **rune** letters that were carved into the World Tree. The runes help guide Odin and give him magical power.

FACT

Odin first appeared as Thor's father in Marvel Comics in 1962. Later, his character appeared in the Thor and The Avengers movie series.

Odin has many magical powers such as
causing people to fall asleep.

Ares has the power to cause great fear in others, including entire armies. This is especially true when he's with his sons Phobos and Deimos. When they go into battle together, they spread fear in their wake. On the flip side, Ares can also inspire amazing courage and strength in his warriors. His leadership helps bring them to victory.

But Ares' greatest power is in his intense emotions and actions in combat. His rage and bloodshed in battle make him nearly unbeatable. No **mortal** weapon can harm Ares. Only magical weapons can injure him.

FACT

Ares appeared as a villain in Marvel Comics beginning in 1966. He opposed Thor, Hercules, and the Avengers. Ares is also one of the main villains in the Percy Jackson book series by Rick Riordan.

Ares inspired courage in his armies and fear in the enemy.

Both Odin and Ares can **shapeshift**. Odin can take the form of various creatures. In one tale he became a snake, a giant, and an eagle. Ares can even turn other people into creatures. For example, he once turned his son into a hawk.

Along with his other abilities, Odin has the power of creation. Before humanity existed, Odin and his brothers killed the cruel giant Ymir. They used Ymir's bones, blood, and flesh to form the universe. Then Odin created the first man and woman from an ash and an elm tree.

Ares can't create things like Odin. But as an Olympian, he is immortal. He can never die and has the gift of eternal youth. He will remain young and handsome forever.

Odin once took the shape of an eagle
to sneak into the home of some giants.

TWO FLAWED GODS

Both Odin and Ares are very powerful. But they aren't perfect. Odin can be pretty selfish. He wants to be the wisest and most powerful god of all, at any cost. He can be sneaky too. In many Norse myths, Odin disguised himself and fooled others by pretending to be someone else.

Odin also doesn't mind stealing. In Norse mythology, he is the leader of the "Wild Hunt." This group of mythical figures rides the sky on cold winter nights. They steal food and other items from houses they pass by.

Odin also stole the **Mead** of Poetry from the giants. This special drink gave him the power to speak and write beautifully.

Norse tales say that Odin often wore a cloak and large
hat to disguise himself.

Ares isn't very popular among the gods. They don't like him because he's always overreacting. He's also disloyal. He knows that Aphrodite is married to his brother Hephaestus. But he dates her anyway, and together they have five children.

Hephaestus

Ares has a nasty temper. For example, Aphrodite once fell in love with a handsome young man named Adonis. Ares grew jealous. He transformed into a boar and killed Adonis with his tusks.

Ares can be impulsive too. He often fights for no reason and gets overly violent. But despite his superhuman strength, he can be defeated. For example, the Aloadae twin giants once trapped him in a bronze jar for thirteen months. Even Athena once wounded Ares by hurling a huge stone at him.

Both Odin and Ares have many strengths, powers, and weaknesses. Considering everything you've learned, who do you think is the greater god?

Odin's End

Although Odin is the main Norse god and is very powerful, he's not immortal. In fact, some sources say he will die one day. The giant wolf Fenrir will eventually kill him at Ragnarök. In Norse mythology, this great battle will happen at the end of the world and most of the gods will die.

ODIN VS. ARES AT A GLANCE

Name: Odin

God of: war, death, wisdom, magic, and poetry

Appearance: a tall, old man with a flowing beard, wearing a blue cloak and a wide-brimmed hat, only has one eye

Weapons: a staff or spear

Strengths: powerful warrior, strategic in war, decides which warriors will win, protects heroes, wise, intelligent

Powers and abilities: can predict the future, practices magic, heals others, communicates with spirits, puts spells on people, shapeshifts, holds the power of creation

Weaknesses: selfish, breaks his word, can be sneaky, dishonest, steals things

Symbols: his two ravens Huginn and Muninn, the magical horse Sleipnir, two wolves named Geri and Freki

Name:	Ares
God of:	war, battle, destruction, violence, rage, and courage
Appearance:	mature warrior dressed for battle, often wears a helmet, usually carries his spear and shield
Weapons:	the spear, sword, and shield
Strengths:	brutality, physical force, skilled with all weapons, courageous, decisive, fearless
Powers and abilities:	influence over others, powerful emotions, can't be injured by mortal weapons, able to shapeshift, immortal with the gift of eternal youth
Weaknesses:	disloyal, unpopular, nasty temper, jealous, impulsive, overly violent, can be defeated
Symbol:	the spear, sword, shield, helmet, chariot, serpent, vulture, and Colchian Dragon

GLOSSARY

brutal (BROO-tuhl)—cruel and violent

divine (dih-VAHYN)—holy or godly in nature

foresight (FOHR-sahyt)—the ability to see or predict the future

mead (MEED)—a winelike drink made from water, honey, and yeast

mortal (MOR-tuhl)—one who has a limited life and eventually dies

Olympian (uh-LIM-pee-uhn)—the main gods and goddesses in Greek mythology who lived on Mount Olympus

pantheon (PAN-thee-on)—all the gods of a certain mythology

primordial (prahy-MOHR-dee-uhl)—existing at or from the beginning of time

ritual (RICH-oo-uhl)—a ceremony involving a set of religious words, objects, and actions that are performed in a specific way

rune (ROON)—a special letter or symbol that is usually carved into wood or stone

shapeshift (SHAYP-shift)—the ability to transform into another form, such as a person, animal, or creature

strategy (STRAT-uh-jee)—a plan of action to achieve a goal

Valkyries (VAL-kuh-reez)—beautiful warrior women in Norse mythology who bring the souls of chosen warriors to Valhalla